THE SEVENTIES

PART TWO

Amarillo (Is This The Way To), 2
Beautiful Sunday, 8
Can You Read My Mind, 5
Chanson D' Amour, 10
Chiquitita, 16
Daughter of Darkness, 13
Day By Day, 20
Diamonds are Forever, 23
Don't It Make My Brown Eyes Blue, 26
Don't Stay Away Too Long, 28
Everything Is Beautiful, 30
The First Time Ever I saw Your Face, 39
From Both Sides Now, 34
Harry, 36
I Don't Want To Put A Hold On You, 44
Isn't She Lovely, 42
Jolene, 49
The Last Farewell, 54
Leaving On A Jet Plane, 60
Lost In France, 57
Love Is Like A Butterfly, 63
New York, New York (Theme From), 66
Nobody Does It Better, 71
Rockin' All Over The World, 74
Save Your Kisses For Me, 77
Sing, 80
Solitaire, 83
Streets Of London, 86
The Tide Is High, 96
Touch Me In The Morning, 91
What Have They Done To My Song, Ma, 100
When A Child Is Born, 112
When You Smile, 106
Where Is The Love, 103
Woman In Love, 109
You Are The Sunshine Of My Life, 114
You Don't Bring Me Flowers, 117
You Light Up My Life, 126
You're A Lady, 129
You're The One That I Want, 122

Edited by PETER FOSS
First published 1990 © International Music Publications
Exclusive Distributors: International Music Publications, Southend Road, Woodford Green, Essex IG8 8HN. England
215-2-624, Order Ref: 17307, ISBN 0 86359 743 2

AMARILLO (Is This The Way To)

Words & Music by
NEIL SEDAKA & HOWARD GREENFIELD

CAN YOU READ MY MIND?

Words by LESLIE BRICUSSE
Music by JOHN WILLIAMS

BEAUTIFUL SUNDAY

Words & Music by
DANIEL BOONE & ROD McQUEEN

9

CHANSON D' AMOUR

Words & Music by
WAYNE SHANKLIN

DAUGHTER OF DARKNESS

Words & Music by
LES REED & GEOFF STEPHENS

VERSE

Wom-an, ———— I can re-mem-ber a wom-an, ————
Hea-ven, ———— we had our own kind of hea-ven, ————

Am

Em

Warm were her kiss-es and ten-der was she, ———— ly-ing there in my
Shar-ing to-geth-er the mag-ic of love ———— in a world of our

Fmaj7   F   Fmaj7   F

CHIQUITITA

Words & Music by
BENNY ANDERSSON & BJORN ULVAEUS

DAY BY DAY

Words & Music by
STEPHEN SCHWARTZ

21

DIAMONDS ARE FOREVER

Words by DON BLACK
Music by JOHN BARRY

24

DON'T IT MAKE MY BROWN EYES BLUE

Words & Music by
RICHARD LEIGH

DON'T STAY AWAY TOO LONG

English lyric by BRYAN BLACKBURN
Music by HENRY MAYER

EVERYTHING IS BEAUTIFUL

Words & Music by
RAY STEVENS

33

FROM BOTH SIDES NOW

Words & Music by
JONI MITCHELL

So ma-ny times I would have done ———— but clouds got in my way.
And if you care don't let them know, ———— don't give your-self a - way.
But some-thing's lost, but some-thing's gained ———— in liv - ing ev - 'ry day.

I've

C   F   Dm   G

looked at {clouds/love/life} FROM BOTH SIDES NOW, from {up and/give and/win and} {down/take,/lose,} and still ——— some-how it's

C   F   C   F   C   F   C

{cloud/love's/life's} ill - u - sions I re-call, I real ——ly——don't know {clouds/love/life} ———————— at ———

Em   F   C   Dm7 (G bass)   G7

(Last time only)

all. ————————— ( ) —————————

C   F   C   F   C   F   C   F   C

HARRY

Words & Music by
CATHERINE HOWE

THE FIRST TIME EVER I SAW YOUR FACE

39

Words & Music by
EWAN MacCOLL

The first time ever I saw your face,

I thought the sun rose in your eyes

2. The first time ever I kissed your mouth
   I felt the earth move in my hand,
   Like the trembling heart of a captive bird
   That was there at my command, my love,
   That was there at my command.

3. The first time ever I lay with you
   And felt your heart so close to mine,
   And I knew our joy would fill the earth
   And last till the end of time, my love.
   The first time ever I saw your face,
   Your face, your face, your face.

ISN'T SHE LOVELY

Words & Music by
STEVIE WONDER

I DON'T WANT TO PUT A HOLD ON YOU

Words & Music by
MICHAEL & BERNI FLINT

JOLENE

Words & Music by
DOLLY PARTON

Fairly bright tempo

52

53

3. You could have your choice of men, but I could never love again.
   He's the only one for me, Jolene.
   I had to have this talk with you,
   My happiness depends on you
   And whatever you decide to do, Jolene.
   (To Chorus)

THE LAST FAREWELL

Words by R A WEBSTER
Music by ROGER WHITTAKER

LOST IN FRANCE

Words & Music by
RONNIE SCOTT & STEVE WOLFE

58

59

LEAVING ON A JET PLANE

Words & Music by
JOHN DENVER

LOVE IS LIKE A BUTTERFLY

Words & Music by
DOLLY PARTON

To Coda

Love is like ____ a but – ter – fly a rare and gen – tle thing.

1. I feel it when you're with me it
2. Your laugh – ter brings me sun – shine,

hap – pens when you kiss me that rare and gen – tle feel – ing
ev – 'ry day is spring-time and I am on – ly hap – py when

that I feel in – side. Your touch is soft and
you are by my side. How pre – cious is this

NEW YORK, NEW YORK (THEME FROM)

Words by FRED EBB
Music by JOHN KANDER

67

NOBODY DOES IT BETTER

Words by CAROLE BAYER SAGER
Music by MARVIN HAMLISCH

73

ROCKIN' ALL OVER THE WORLD

Words & Music by
JOHN FOGERTY

76

SAVE YOUR KISSES FOR ME

Words & Music by
TONY HILLER, MARTIN LEE & LEE SHERIDAN

78

SING

Words & Music by
JOE RAPOSO

81

SOLITAIRE

Words & Music by
NEIL SEDAKA & PHILIP CODY

STREETS OF LONDON

Words & Music by
RALPH McTELL

1

mind.

D   A/C#   Bm   A7(sus)   A7

2

mind.

D   A(C#bass)   Bm   F#m(Abass)

G   Em/G E9/G#   A7(sus 4)   A7

VERSE

2. In the all ___ night ca-fé   at a quart-er past ___ e - lev - en

3. Have you seen ___ the old man   out - side the sea - man's miss-ion,

D   A(C#bass)   Bm   F#m(Abass)

89

TOUCH ME IN THE MORNING

Words by RON MILLER
Music by MICHAEL MASSER

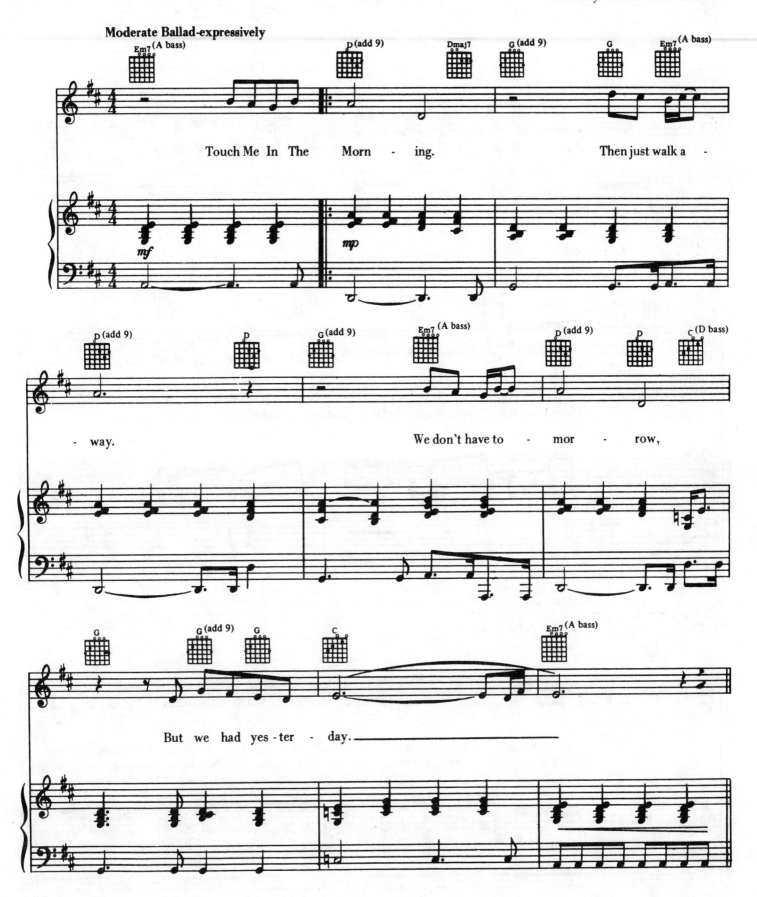

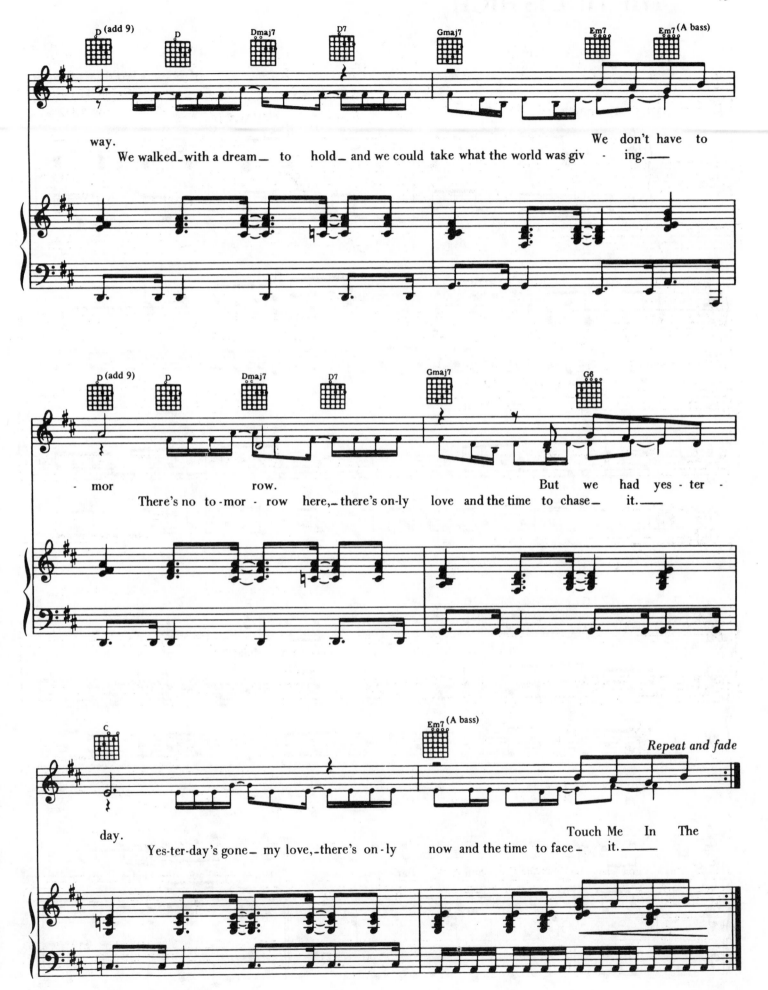

THE TIDE IS HIGH

Words & Music by
JOHN HOLT

The tide is high but I'm hold - in' on,
I'm gon - na be your num - ber one.
I'm— not the kind-a girl

98

WHAT HAVE THEY DONE TO MY SONG, MA

Words & Music by
MELANIE SAFKA

5. Maybe it'll all be alright Ma, maybe it'll all be O. K.
Well, if the people are buying tears I'll be rich someday, Ma,
Look what they've done to my song.

6. Ils ont changé ma chanson, Ma, Ils ont changé ma chanson,
C'est la seule chose que je peux faire et ce n'est pas bon ma,
Ils ont changé ma chanson.

7 Look what they've done to my song Ma,
Look what they've done to my song Ma,
Well they tied it up in a plastic bag, turned it upside down, Ma,
Look what they've done to my song.

8. Look what thay've done to my song, Ma,
Look what they've done to my song,
Well it's the only thing that I could do half right, and it's turning out all wrong, Ma,
Look what they've done to my song.

WHERE IS THE LOVE

Words & Music by
RALPH MacDONALD & WILLIAM SALTER

WHEN YOU SMILE

Words & Music by
WILLIAM SALTER & RALPH MACDONALD

WOMAN IN LOVE

Words & Music by
DOMINIC BUGATTI & FRANK MUSKER

WHEN A CHILD IS BORN

Words by FRED JAY
Music by ZACAR

113

YOU ARE THE SUNSHINE OF MY LIFE

Words & Music by
STEVIE WONDER

YOU DON'T BRING ME FLOWERS

Words by NEIL DIAMOND,
Music by NEIL DIAMOND, MARILYN BERGMAN & ALAN BERGMAN

YOU'RE THE ONE THAT I WANT

Words & Music by
JOHN FARRAR

YOU LIGHT UP MY LIFE

Words & Music by
JOE BROOKS

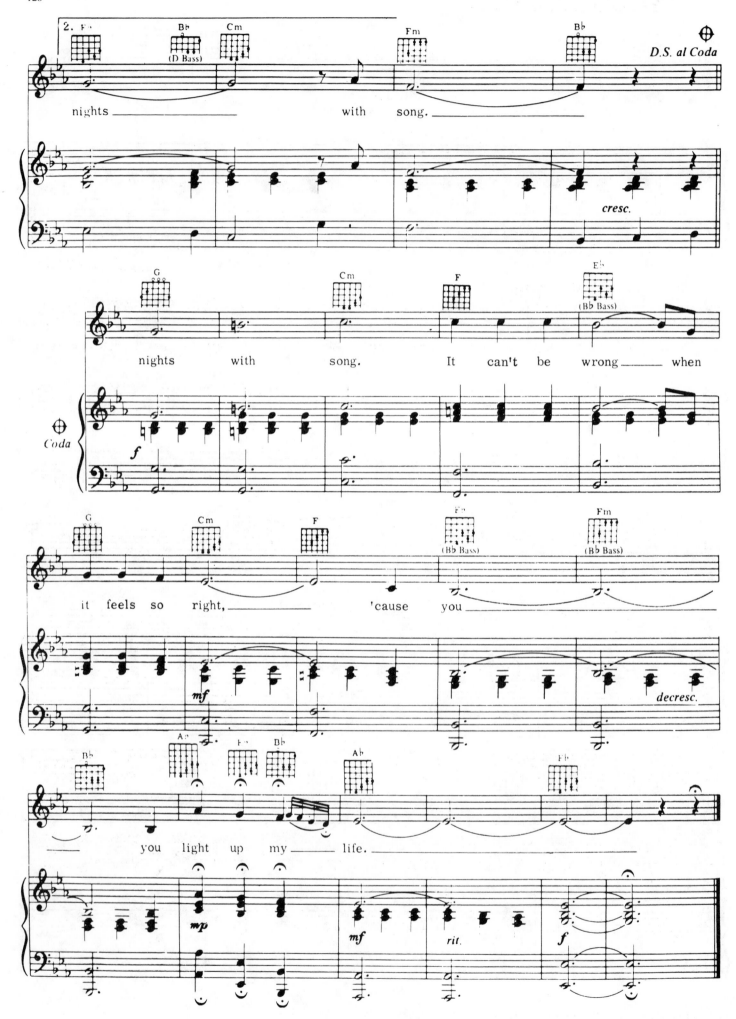

YOU'RE A LADY

Words & Music by
PETER SKELLERN

Moderato

(Verse) Freely(with expression)

Now the ev'-ning has come to a close and I've had my last dance with

you. On to the emp-ty streets we go

and it might be my last chance with you; so I might as well get it

2. Hard to answer, - yes, I agree - but then I've got to know;
I'm not asking you to marry me - just a little love to show.
Oh, I know I could make you happy, so the things I have to say
Won't wait until another day.